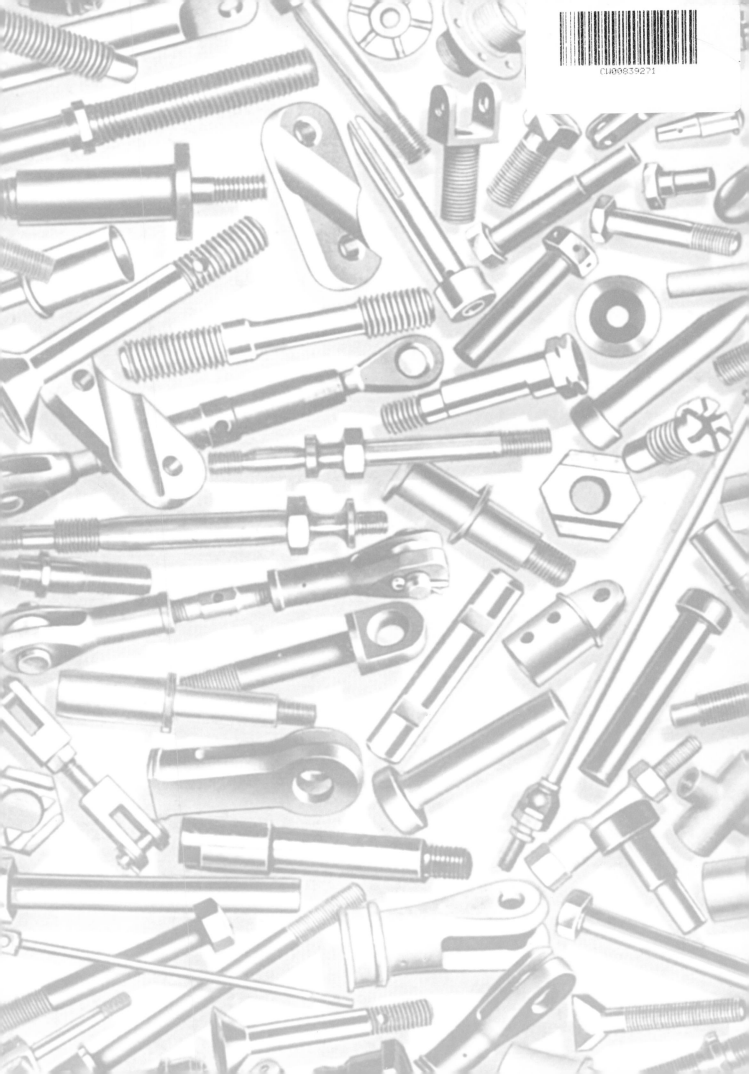

Previous page: Some of the aircraft components made by Rubery Owen in the 1950s

RUBERY, OWEN & Co.

TELEGRAMS & CABLEGRAMS
"ROOFS, DARLASTON"
A.B.C. CODE 5TH EDITION

TELEPHONE No.
DARLASTON 87
PRIVATE BRANCH EXCHANGE

REGISTERED   TRADE MARK

CONTRACTORS TO
WAR OFFICE,
ADMIRALTY AND
CROWN AGENTS

WORKS   OFFICES

ENGINEERS.

Darlaston, South Staffs.
ENGLAND.

ADDRESS REPLY TO
No. 1 MOTOR FRAME DEPT.

MEMORIES OF
RUBERY OWEN

COMPILED BY R. J. OWEN

Memories of Rubery Owen
Published by
Neate Publishing Ltd
33 Downside Road
Winchester
Hampshire
SO22 5LT
01962 841479
www.neatepublishing.co.uk
sales@neatepublishing.co.uk

ISBN: 1-903634-40-7
ISBN: 978-1-903634-40-7

Printed in the United Kingdom by Bishops of Portsmouth.

Designed by Bernard Fallon Associates

Special thanks to members of the Owen family for use of material from
their private photographic collection.
We would also like to thank the following:

   Aston Studios
   Austin Motor Company
   Birmingham Post and Mail
   Express and Star
   S. Griffiths
   R. Hawthorne
   Keystone Press
   Mazeppa marketing services
   C. Mason
   Morland Braithwaite
   Motor Sport
   C. Pinson
   S. Phillips
   N. Stanforth
   E. Sarginson
   The Midland Press Agency
   The Rover Company
   E. Welch, and all the Rubery Owen in-house photographers both past
   and present who recorded the events throughout so many years.

Cover photos:
Stores of unfinished products, 1920s

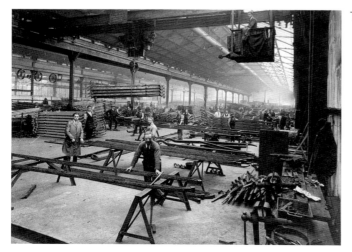

The Assembly Shop, 1920s

FOREWORD

Carl Chinn MBE

Noah Hingley of Netherton; the Manders of Wolverhampton; Joseph Lucas and George Cadbury of Birmingham; the Chances of Smethwick; John Wilkinson of Bilston; the Lloyds of Wednesbury; the Kenricks of West Bromwich – just some of the dynamic and forceful individuals and families of the West Midlands who have made their mark upon the industrial and civic life of our region. They are folk whose achievements bestride our manufacturing and municipal history. Each of them was tied to a specific place and to a particular product, be it anchors or chocolate, bicycle lamps or glass, iron or paints, yet their reputations were spread wide across the developed world through their ingenuity, inventiveness, entrepreneurship, hard work and talent. Their wares brought fame to the towns in which their factories stood, but they did not stand alone, for each town and village across the Black Country and almost each district in Birmingham boasted a business or trade that reached out to the four corners of the globe: Walsall with its saddlery, Willenhall with its locks, Hockley with its jewellery and Darlaston with its nuts and bolts of the famed Guest Keen and Nettlefold's.

One of the smaller Black Country towns, Darlaston punched massively above its weight on the industrial stage and that it did so was not just down to GKN – it owed as much to a company that continues to pride itself on its bond with the Black Country. That firm is Rubery Owen. In the late nineteenth century it pushed itself into the limelight through its innovation, design and quality products, thrusting to notice a long-established business. Back in 1834 a Jabez Rubery had been a gun lock filer, screw turner and gun lock maker. Fifty years on the brothers J. T. and T. W. Rubery had started a factory in Booth Street for making light steel roof work, fencing, gates and the occasional bridge. Later T. W. Rubery left the business, and in 1893 his brother went into partnership with Alfred Ernest Owen.

A young engineer of talent, foresight and determination, Ernest as he was known, transformed the company. Alert to the rise of new industries and to the potential for supplying them with new products, he oversaw the making of an award-winning chassis frame for a car made from rolled sections and solid round steel bars.

In 1910 Ernest became sole owner and with his acute vision he added an aviation department, so allowing Rubery Owen to supply small aircraft components in the First World War. By that time, his company was also making car wheels and had taken over Chains Limited of Wednesbury and Nuts and Bolts Ltd of Darlaston as well as two Birmingham businesses.

Alfred Ernest Owen died in 1929. He was followed ably by his two sons, Sir Alfred and Ernest. They led a highly skilled, motivated workforce that helped the people of Darlaston withstand the ravages of the Depression of the 1930s and which played a vital role in the Second World War. Rubery Owen's structural department at Darlaston was responsible for building shadow factories, aircraft hangers, Bailey bridges, tank-landing craft and components for the Mulberry Harbours that were so essential to the success of the Normandy Landings. During the same period, the motor-frame department made gun carriages, projectiles, mines and bomb-trolleys; the motor wheel department produced instrument containers, bomb carriers, anti-submarine weapons, bomb tails and much more; whilst the aviation department turned out nuts and bolts for aircraft.

This book of wonderful, evocative photos highlights the importance of Rubery Owen, the powerful tie that draws together the Owen family and our region, and the vital role played by a host of dedicated workers. Rubery Owen is a name that is as proud and significant as any of the great manufacturers of the West Midlands. That it gained this distinction is because of a remarkable partnership between the Owens, their workers and the people of Darlaston.

THE CONTRIBUTORS

Charlie Pinson

Charlie worked at R.O. Darlaston from leaving school to become Engineering Director. For many years he was associated with the company's pantomime productions and fire brigade service and tournaments. He provided pictures from his own library and was invaluable in supplying names of employees and information relating to the company's products. Sadly aged 82 he has not lived to see the finished book. It is hoped that he would have approved. Certainly, his company and his jokes will be missed, not only by his fellow compilers, but by everyone else who knew him.

Roy Hawthorne

From school Roy joined the company and completed his engineering apprenticeship. After National Service with the R.A.F, he rejoined the company working as a photographic engineer and obtained qualifications with the British Institute of Professional Photography, he lectured part -time on the subject of photography at local colleges. He has not only supplied many of the photographs in this book but has provided invaluable help in collating them.

Stan Griffiths

Stan, his wife and his father (David Griffiths, who started in 1914), represent over one hundred years service at the firm. Stan was closely involved with the agricultural plough dept. and worked in other tool rooms ending his time at R.O. based up at the King's Hill factory. From the late 40s to the early 60s he took numerous shots of all the company's social events. He too, has kindly donated many of his own personal photographs. He is still adding to his collection, particularly those of Darlaston, being a long term serving member of the local history society.

Jim Owen

Jim is the younger brother to David and John. He joined the company on leaving school as a student commercial apprentice, on its completion he joined the Training Department and was responsible for graduate and student training. He later became Estates Director responsible for the Holding's company land and property. He has worked tirelessly to compile this publication.

INTRODUCTION

This book is a celebration in photographs of the people who worked at Rubery Owen from the turn of the 19th to the late 20th century. It shows how a factory grew from very small beginnings, making iron and steel fencing and small bridges, to being at the very heart of the growth of UK manufacturing, in structural steelwork, metal fabrications and the motor component industry.

Rubery Owen began in 1884 in Darlaston, a small Black Country town now part of Walsall, when Mr J. T. Rubery who had been working with his brother, decided to branch out on his own in a small steel constructional business. He quickly realised that he needed a younger partner and advertised the position in 1893. The advertisement was noticed by Alfred Owen of Woodhey, Wrexham, who had apprenticed his son, Alfred Ernest Owen, to a foundry up in Deeside. Wanting also to branch out on his own instead of joining the firm that his father had run in Wrexham, A. E. Owen armed with some of his father's money went down to meet Mr Rubery at the Victoria Works, Darlaston. The two men hit it off immediately and so at the age of 24, A. E. Owen joined Mr Rubery as his partner in 1893.

Ernest, as he was known in the family, was a very good practical engineer and soon saw the opportunities that lay ahead in motor cars and the need for a strong supporting component industry. The first venture was chassis frames for cars and then trucks, followed soon after by wheels for passenger cars, axle housings for both cars and trucks and nuts and bolts for the vehicle and aviation industries.

J. T Rubery retired in 1910 and sold out his interest to A. E. Owen. The firm was growing rapidly. A. G. B. Owen took over from his father in 1930 after his sudden and premature death and, together with his younger brother Ernest, expanded the Darlaston Company from some 1700 employees in 1929 to over 5000 by 1969. Ernest died in 1967 and in 1969 A.G.B.O., at the age of 61, suffered a stroke forcing him into early retirement. His sons David and John now took over the company and with their younger brother Jim are still running Rubery Owen Holdings as it is known today— three generations stretching well over 100 years.

There are two strong threads that run through this photographic record, namely the products and the people who made them.

Some of the most important products were landmarks of structural engineering; for example: – the west stand at Twickenham Rugby Football Ground, the stadium for Wolverhampton Wanderers built in the 1930s, the flyover at Oxford Circus when the new Victoria Line was built in the 1960s, a similar structure for the Warwick/Coventry Road in Birmingham and in 1952 the College of Technology at Birmingham (now Aston University) which was opened by HM The Queen.

Even more significantly, Rubery Owen pioneered production engineering techniques in the automotive components industry, building the first independent steel chassis frame for Daimler in 1898, developing the cold pressing of sidemembers for commercial vehicles in the 1920s with a 1500 ton 'upstroking' Wilkins & Mitchell press, nicknamed the 'backbreaker', which now stands proudly outside the Black Country Living Museum. In 1938 a sideloading 2000 ton British Clearing Press had been installed and in the 1960s a 4000 ton 'Weingarten' sideloading press, the biggest in the country for doing the heaviest and longest chassis frames up to 42 feet in

length. In the meantime hot pressings for frames with particularly difficult rear end wheel arches were supplied for bus chassis.

Another interesting development was the Scott patent rear axle for light commercial vehicles which enabled a seamless tube to be expanded through a hot press to house the gearing for a rear axle. Another axle development was the welded heavy axle comprising two halves welded together. Rubery Owen also pioneered the friction welding of the hub ends for brake and wheel assembly.

Yet another challenge was the complex front sub frame for Alex Issigonis's famous 'mini', where all the multi parts were pressed from coiled strip and then welded together. Then there was the development of the 'ribbed' RO-Style steel wheel which, amongst others, was fitted to the elegant Ford Capri and MG sports cars.

Rubery Owen also built the chassis frame for the first pioneering British Formula I Grand Prix car, the BRM, and then went on to run the team, finally winning the World Championship in 1962 with an all-British made car driven by Graham Hill.

This book shows how people worked and how the factory and its associated activities became the dominant feature in many people's lives – how factories became larger and equipment heavier and stronger to push forward the boundaries of keeping pace with world demand.

However in keeping pace with the world demand, the company saw the importance of its employees as being the key to success. One of the interesting features at Rubery Owen in the 1920s and 30s was the naming of roads within the main factory after long serving employees –

namely Buckley, Guy, Green, Drayton, Rock, Fletcher, Foster, Westwood, Lee, Downs, Freeman. These were ordinary employees, some becoming managers, others just spending a lifetime with the same firm. Of course there were many others who deserved similar recognition, had there been sufficient roads to name!

There are many examples of how the welfare of employees was considered over the years. A. E. Owen was a founder member of the Industrial Welfare Society (later the Industrial Society) and the company was the first in the Midlands to provide a canteen for its workpeople. Recreation facilities were built as well for bowls, billiards and tennis and were always well used for pleasure as well as matches and competitions.

As can be seen in the photographs, women featured strongly, particularly in light engineering such as the production of bolts and nuts and light pressings. Their nimble finger work particularly suited the process and there was great camaraderie along the line of working machines. During the war, a nursery was formed at Rubery Owen to enable women to continue to work, while their children were safely looked after with qualified nurses in attendance. Women workers featured strongly in the Black Country where the first ever 'Women's Institute' for workers was built in 1911 and is now being moved to the Black Country Living Museum for posterity.

Immediately after the Second World War, houses were built and rented out cheaply to attract young married couples into the firm, many coming from the North East and Wales to join what was the 'hey-day' of British manufacturing in the late 1950s and early 1960s. In 1949, the Sons of Rest workshop was started for employees retiring from the

shop floor. Many felt suddenly they were being thrown on the scrap heap and the workshop not only enabled them to continue light work as and when it suited them, but aided production departments in the main factory with the supply of some awkward short run small components. Later in the 1950s, Preparation for Retirement courses, the first ever in the country for industry, were started to help people to prepare and adjust for their retirement.

Apprenticeship schemes, both commercial and engineering, were started after the Second World War. The engineers had their own training workshop to learn basic skills for the first year and then went out to different departments to be apprenticed to experienced workers. The scheme was a by-word in the Black Country. Owners of local firms sent their sons to learn their trade away from being the 'gaffer's son'. The training could get you a job anywhere but most were taken up in the ever expanding departments. These skills and knowledge lasted a life time.

The book is deliberately chronological so it is easy to picture how working life developed over the years.

It also shows how the working week was not all that mattered to people who worked. Apart from the necessity to bring home money for the family, there were other things to appreciate and enjoy. Sports and Social occasions were high on each person's agenda. There was friendly rivalry on Sports Days, inter-departmental bowls, football, cricket matches and other sports; horticultural and flower shows, a chess club and photographic competitions. There were also drama groups, pantomimes, works dances with famous bands such as Joe Loss and Cyril Stapleton, Christmas parties for the children and many other social events. There was a doctor and dentist's surgery as well

as the nursery for young children of working parents. Friendships were made that lasted a lifetime and many a marriage took place between people who worked within the company.

Rubery Owen was fortunate in that it had good qualified photographers. Their work ranged from producing prints as large as 15 feet long and 10 feet wide for international exhibitions, photographing company products for catalogues, which were distributed worldwide, and scientific photography for the Research and Development Department, such as photo-elasticity tests and various UV light application techniques. Of course they also attended social events, sports days and family events, which were recorded in the Company newspaper, The Owen News.

We are lucky in having this photographic record of all that went on at Rubery Owen (Darlaston) over the last hundred years. It has been difficult to make choices and many photographs have been left out through lack of space. However we hope the book will be an interesting record of a Black Country firm that still lives to tell the story of one of its most important workplaces and continues to develop new products for the future.

David Owen OBE
Group Chairman

1893-1930

The two Partners of Rubery and Co.
Alfred Ernest Owen on the left and
John Tunner Rubery on the right in
1899.

Alfred Ernest Owen's wedding to Florence Lucy, eldest daughter of George Beech, of Jesmond Grove Edgbaston on June 27th 1900 at St. George's Church.

The Rubery family in the garden of their home at Blockall (circa 1900).
John Rubery and his wife Kate were married in 1881.
Miss Edith Rubery (1892-1977) is on the swing with her elder sisters Mary, Kathleen, Gladys and Marguerite.

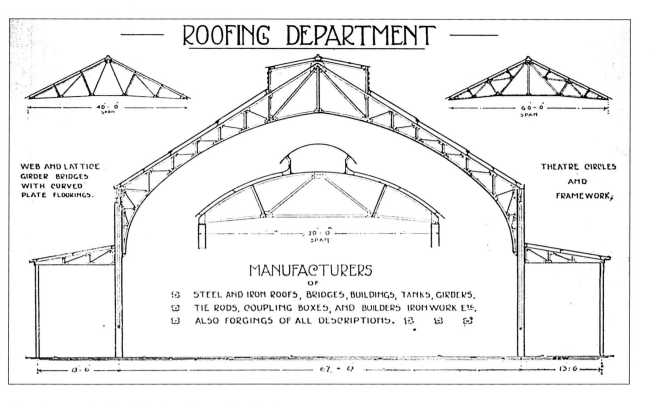

Advertisements for the original roofing and fencing departments.

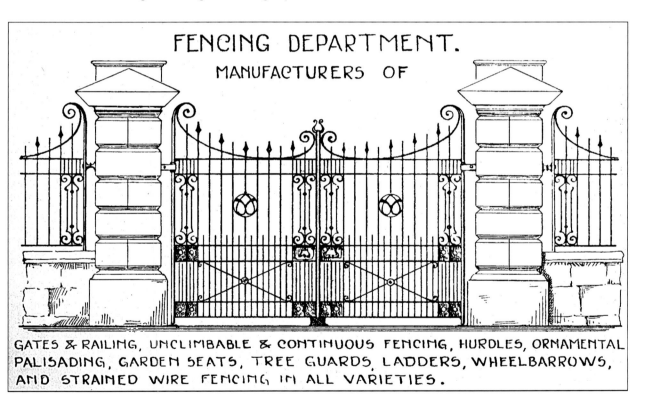

Trading under the name
'Rubery & Co.' the partners
would have considered this
job as substantial.
In 1905 the style of the firm
was changed to 'Rubery
Owen and Co.'

The Darlaston Manufacturers' Annual Excursion in 1898 to the Cotswolds.
A.E. Owen is at the end of the middle row on the far right. J.T. Rubery is beside him, hands crossed with a straw hat on.

Front row (left to right): Billy Bott, George Gutteridge, Charlie Duckham, Frank Wyers, Jack Hadland, Joe Brookes, Alf Brookes.
Middle row: David Chew, Jnr., Harry Hunt, Billy Horton, David Chew, Snr., Ben Bott, Tom Horne, Jack Foster, Johnny O'Connor.
Back row: Harry Firman, Almond Price, William Franklin, Tom Jones, Billy Giles, Ponto Bagguley, Harry Hollinshead, Joby Kemp, Tommy Owen, Fred Lappage *(behind)*, Jack Critch, Jim Richards *(behind)*, Sam Wyers, Bob Wells *(behind)*.

The Blacksmiths' Shop.

A.E. Owen purchased a series of presses up to the First World War. This 1500 ton 'upstroking' Wilkins and Mitchell chassis press built in 1913 nick-named the 'backbreaker', is now situated at the Black Country Living Museum.

Advertisements from the opening pages of the 1907 Catalogue, proudly displaying the Richmond Medal and the trade associations the company had joined.

The earliest record we have of the Engineering Department, (circa 1905).

The hydraulic presses and patent gas furnace used in the manufacture of motor car frames, sides and crossbars of all descriptions. (circa 1910)

The Assembling Shop including the Works Office.

The main offices and the original Workman's Institute constructed of best Ruabon brick with stone corner facings opened in 1912 at the junction of Queen Street and Booth Street, Darlaston.

The work's clock tower entrance and additional offices opposite were also built in 1912. C.W.D Joynson designed all the buildings.

The trade mark set in the mosaic floor of the entrance hall reminded all office staff of the company's name!

The company was one of the first to provide recreation grounds for employees.
The pavilion bowling green and tennis court opened on 24th May 1913. Viewed here towards Willenhall Road.

These advertisements from an early catalogue indicate the firm's increasing involvement with the motor component trade as well as aviation accessories.

WE REPAIR FRAMES

MANUFACTURERS
of
MOTOR VEHICLE FRAMES
of every description
also

AXLE CASES, BRA...
CLUTCH DRUMS, TOP...
and
STEP BRACKETS,

BOLTS AND ...
MADE SPECIALLY FOR MOTOR ...

RUBERY, O...
DARLASTON. S...
TELEPHONE 87. TELE...

PLEASE ADDRESS ALL COMMUNIC...

RUBERY, OWEN & Co. DARLASTO...

Aeroplane Department.

CONTRACTORS TO
ADMIRALTY, WAR OFFICE AND CROWN AGENTS.

Aeroplane Accessories
of every description.

RUBERY, OWEN & Co.'s PATENT RELEASE GEARS.
"FOX'S" PATENT WIRE BENDING PLIERS.
"SHORT" PATENT WIRE STRAINERS.
SPECIAL STRAINERS FOR R.A.F.
ORDINARY STRAINERS, (BRASS BODIES).
STEEL LOCK-NUT STRAINERS.
FORKED END STRAINERS.
SPECIAL LARGE STEEL STRAINERS.
EYEBOLTS IN VARIOUS KINDS OF STEEL.
STEEL CABLE ENDS.
QUICK RELEASE BOLTS.
SPECIAL BOLTS FITTED WITH LUBRICATORS.
METRIC THREAD BOLTS AND NUTS.
B.A. BOLTS AND NUTS.
ENGINE PLATES AND HOUSINGS.
TUBULAR FRAMEWORK.
FUSELAGE ANGLE PLATES, ETC., ETC.

> **WE MAKE BOLTS AND NUTS**
> SPECIALLY FOR
> **MOTOR CAR MANUFACTURERS.**

Please address all communications to No. 1 Aero. Department.

ILLUSTRATED CATALOGUE OF AEROPLANE ACCESSORIES SENT FREE
ON APPLICATION.

The new 'stand alone' Canteen and Institute opened for business on Saturday 16th August 1919. A.E. Owen's elder son, Alfred Owen cut the ribbon. It was built on the original recreation ground but the area lost was immediately replaced by the purchase of adjacent land.

The kitchen boasted the latest cooking apparatus providing meals for the downstairs mess room, which is thought to have seated 600.

The Central Office staff photographed on the tennis court adjoining the main canteen (circa 1919).

Delivery of chassis frames from the works (Early1920s).
The cobbles and tramway lines suggest the road was in the Bullstake area of Darlaston.

The General Office showing early comptometer machines in use.

The Typists' Office (note the electricity supplied-connections to the dictaphones).

Careful scrutiny of the calendar hanging in the Drawing Office dates this to November 1925.
It advertises The Glacier Metal Co. Ltd. of Alperton Wembley.

The Drawing Office.

The original works laboratory and test house included a surgery for employees. The building was later demolished and the site became part of the Hot Press Department.

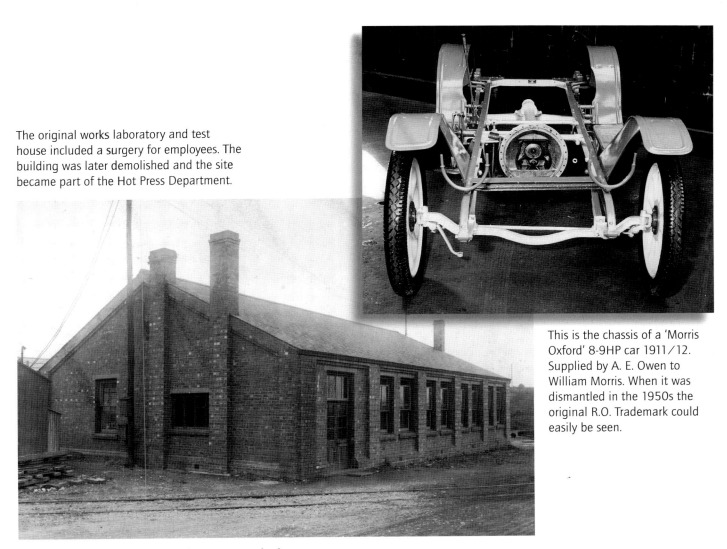

This is the chassis of a 'Morris Oxford' 8-9HP car 1911/12. Supplied by A. E. Owen to William Morris. When it was dismantled in the 1950s the original R.O. Trademark could easily be seen.

A rather concerned patient receiving treatment in the surgery.

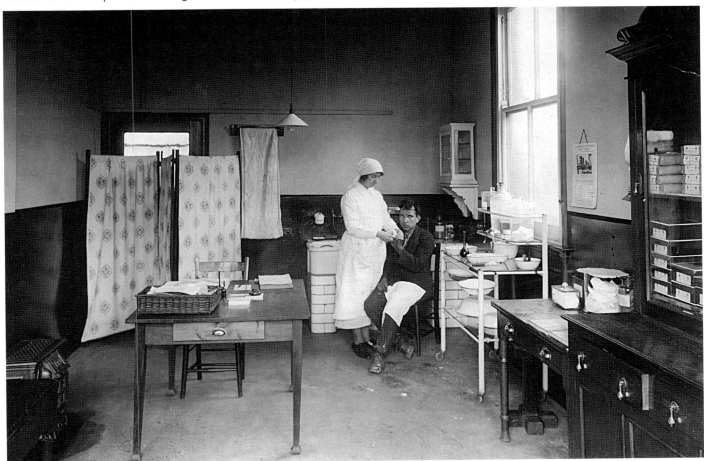

An aerial view of the works and offices in the early 1920s.

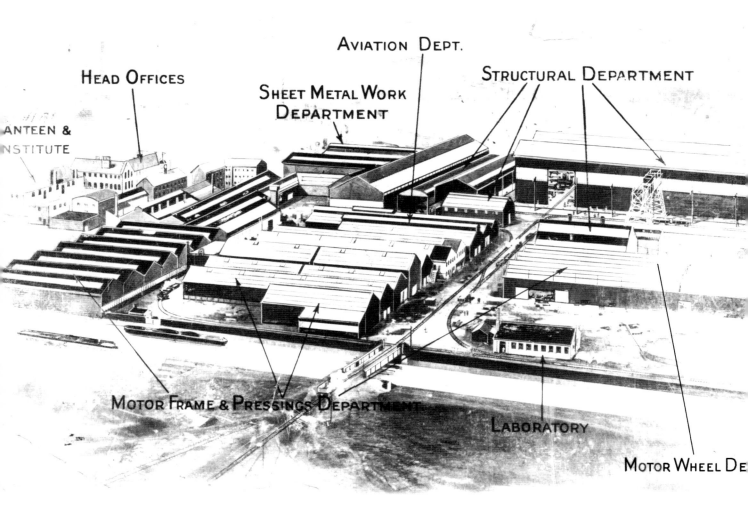

HEAD OFFICES

AVIATION DEPT.

SHEET METAL WORK
DEPARTMENT

STRUCTURAL DEPARTMENT

ANTEEN &
NSTITUTE

MOTOR FRAME & PRESSINGS DEPARTMENT

LABORATORY

MOTOR WHEEL DE

A.E. Owen proudly standing at the centre of his workforce during the difficult years of the depression and general strike, (circa 1920s)

The drilling screwing and facing section of the Aviation Department in 1925. Note the high number of female employees in this area
The cast iron stoves were a welcome form of heating, found in all departments.

The Assembly Shop.

Stores of unfinished products.

The Hot Pressing Shop showing the No. 3 bay.

A 1920s view of the Sheet Metal Department.

The Erecting Shop with its high overhead cranes, later to become the Structural Department.

Again female workers feature in the new Motor Wheel Department which started production in 1924.

THE MIDLAND ADVERTISER AND

BOWLING LEAGUE CHAMPIONS.

Darlaston Team's Dual Success.

There was a record gathering at the Victoria Works Canteen, Darlaston, on Saturday evening, when the members of the Rubery Owen and Wellman-Smith Owen Bowling Club held their eleventh annual dinner and distribution of prizes. Apart from the numbers present, there was another record, inasmuch as Rubery Owen's had won both the first and second divisions of the Wolverhampton and District Bowling League.

Councillor A. E. Owen, principal of the firm and president of the club, occupied the chair, and was supported among others by Messrs. C. Partridge, G. Buckley, H. Price, H. Sinnett, W. Hill (Welfare supervisor), W. Kirton, H. Wallens, A. F. Green, J. K. Hunt (Chillington Tool Co.), T. Matthews (secretary of the Bowling League), J. Desborough (chairman of the committee), B. Grainger (vice-chairman), and J. L. Foster (secretary fo Rubery Owen's Bowling Club).

There were about 200 present at the dinner, but splendid arrangements had been made by the canteen staff and everyone was served in an expeditous manner.

SECRETARY'S REPORT.

PRESENTATION TO COUNCILLOR OWEN.

Mr. W. Hill then performed a pleasing ceremony. He said, as they knew, that was the eleventh annual dinner of the Bowling Club; therefore they had been connected with Welfare sports activities for some years. Welfare work was set up by Mr. Owen before it became general, and it came as a surprise to many. Since then, however, it had been emulated by many firms in the district. During the eleven years Mr. Owen had presided at many prize distributions and many prizes had been due to his bounty. (Hear, hear.) For some years past Mr. Owen had had to bear a heavy burden for besides illhealth he had a lot of business worries. They all hoped, however, that he had seen the end of both business and health troubles. Mr. Hill then mentioned that they wished to show their appreciation to Mr. Owen and thank him for his continued kindness to the different sections of the Welfare Committee. It was with pleasure that he asked Mr. Owen to accept the gift which had been provided (a handsome smoker's cabinet), and when he looked at it and used it, he hoped he would remember that he held the gratitude and esteem of 1,220 workpeople. (Loud applause.)

VALUE OF WELFARE WORK.

Probably taken on November 29th 1924 at the 11th annual dinner of the Bowling Club. Members of R.O. and Wellman Smith Owen Engineering Corp. Ltd (founded in 1919, A.E.Owen was Chairman). The R.O. Club members won championship honours in both sections of the Wolverhampton Works Bowling league, their captain J.T. Green, had won eight medals since joining and Z. Clay had represented Staffordshire in county matches. A.E. Owen always presided at such events and personally donated many of the prizes.

Above
Mr and Mrs A.E. Owen entertained 2000 guests to help celebrate the 21st birthday of their eldest son A.G.B. Owen. The large marquee was placed on the Recreation Grounds on Saturday, April 6th 1929.

Right
The last time A.E. Owen formally addressed some of his workforce was at the Annual Dinner of the Bowling Club on Saturday, November 23rd 1929. Here he spoke of the great value of health as compared to wealth.

On the following Monday he was taken ill, with a reoccurrence of old problem. Five years earlier he had undergone an operation for a duodenal ulcer now he had to enter a Sutton Coldfield Nursing Home for treatment again. Despite giving an upbeat message for Christmas buoyed up by numerous gifts, flowers and good wishes, he perhaps feared the worst by adding his personal message *'Keep the Flag Flying'*. He died on the 30th December 1929.

T O   M Y   E M P L O Y E E S :
==

ALTHOUGH ILLNESS PREVENTS ME FROM BEING WITH YOU PERSONALLY AT DARLASTON THIS CHRISTMASTIDE, I HAVE YOU ALL IN MY THOUGHTS, AND WANT TO EXPRESS THE SINCERE WISH THAT EACH AND EVERY ONE OF YOU WILL SPEND A BRIGHT AND HAPPY CHRISTMAS, AND THAT THE NEW YEAR WILL BRING US ALL BUSY TIMES AND A GOOD MEASURE OF PROSPERITY.

I AM PLEASED TO SAY MY CONDITION IS IMPROVING.

A.E. Owen
....
AT DR. BOYD'S NURSING HOME,
WENTWORTH LODGE, FOUR OAKS,
SUTTON COLDFIELD.

DECEMBER 24TH 1929.

--------o0o--------

"Keep the flag flying".

FUNERAL SERVICE OF THE LATE MR. A.E. OWEN at the PARISH CHURCH, SUTTON COLDFIELD, JAN.4TH, 1930.

Interment at Cemetery.

TRAINS.   Special Train will leave WILLENHALL -
                                    DARLASTON   -   10.55 a.m.
                                    PLECK   -   11.0 a.m.
                                    WALSALL   -   11.3 a.m.
                                                           11.8 a.m.

           Arriving Sutton Park Station 11.28. a.m.
           and return at 2.15 p.m. from Sutton Park Station.

TICKETS.   Tickets will be distributed to-day by Heads of Staff
           and Foremen to those who have sent in their names.

           Messrs. H. Day and W. Franklin will meet TRAIN at
           SUTTON PARK STATION, and shew the way to the CHURCH.

SEATING   Messrs. W.T. Thornhill, A.R.Wynn, R.W. Downs,
ARRANGEMENTS H.Sinnott, V.V. Powell, J.A. Glover, E.J.Gurmin,
IN CHURCH.   E.C.Coupland, W.Gill, H.Secker, W.Hill,
           W.Tildesley, E.Holberry, W.Robinson, E.Jones,
           T.Cumpston, R.O. Buckley will assist Church
           Wardens in conducting congregation to seats.

           Seating accommodation in the CHURCH may be insufficient
           for our numbers, and while every effort will be made
           to provide room for all, it is hoped, should any be
           unable to enter the Church, they will line up on
           either side of the Church Drive ready to take part
           in the procession to the Cemetery.

PROCESSION After the Service the Congregation will remain
TO CEME-   standing while the cortege leaves the Church. Then
TERY.   the congregation is requested to follow - four abreast
           to the Cemetery gates, which are 5 minutes walk from
           the Church.

A lucky survivor from the family papers damaged in a fire.

SPECIALISTS IN COMPLETE FACTORY BUILDINGS.

ON LISTS OF, AND

...S TO, THE BRITISH ADMIRALTY, WAR OFFICE, AIR MINISTRY & CROWN AGENTS FOR THE COLONIES, INDIA OFFICE & LEADING BRITISH & FOREIGN RAILWAYS.

SIDING: L.M.& S.R. NEAREST PASSENGER STATION, DARLASTON, (L.M.& S.R.) ¾ MILE.

TELEPHONES:
...RLASTON: 130 (P.B.Ex.)
LONDON: HOLBORN 6306 & 7.
BIRMINGHAM: CENTRAL 3092.

ESTABLISHED 1884.

TELEGRAMS & CABLEGRAMS:
RUBEROWEN, DARLASTON.
RUBEROWEN WESTCENT, LONDON.
RUBEROWEN, BIRMINGHAM.

COMMUNICATIONS
FIRM — NOT TO
INDIVIDUALS.

CODES
A.B.C. 5ᵀᴴ EDITION.
BENTLEYS.
WESTERN UNION.

RUBERY, OWEN & Cº.

(PROPRIETOR: A.E. OWEN)

BRIDGES, PIERS, JETTIES, TANKS, ROOFS, BUILDINGS;
MOTOR VEHICLE CHASSIS FRAMES AND COMPONENT PARTS;
WINGS, BONNETS, DASHES, LUGGAGE GRIDS, PETROL TANKS, ETC;
WHEELS (PLEASURE CAR AND COMMERCIAL VEHICLE); TRADE ENAMELLING;
GENERAL PRESSED WORK FOR THE MOTOR AND ALLIED TRADES;
BRIGHT STEEL BOLTS AND NUTS, ETC; BRIGHT DRAWN STEEL;
AIRCRAFT FRAMEWORK, STRUTS, WINGS, TURNBUCKLES, EYEBOLTS, ETC;

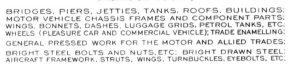

LONDON:
IMPERIAL BUILDINGS,
56, KINGSWAY, W.C.2.

CONSTRUCTIONAL ENGINEERS & MANUFACTURERS.

DARLASTON.

SOUTH STAFFS, ENGLAND.

BIRMINGHAM:
NORWICH UNION CHAMBERS
CONGREVE STREET.

YOUR REFERENCE   OUR REFERENCE

7th January 1930.

Dear Sir(s),

     We regret to announce the death of our Principal,
Mr. A.E. Owen, which sad event occurred on the 30th ultimo.

     Mr. Owen's illness spread over a few weeks, and, although
it was realised his condition was serious, there was great hope of his
recovery.

     The business will be carried on under the same Management
and on the principles established by Mr. Owen; and in accordance with
his wishes his two Sons are entering the business.

     Mr. Owen took a deep personal interest in his Works, and
was known personally to numbers of our customers. We are hoping that
his Sons will be able to take his place in that connection also, and
that the pleasant relationships which existed between us during
Mr. Owen's lifetime, will be continued in the future. We assure
you that no effort will be spared on our part to maintain them.

          Yours faithfully,
     p.p. RUBERY, OWEN & CO.,

          Geo. H. Buckley,   )
) Joint General
          Chas. E. Partridge,   ) Managers.

DEATH OF MR. A. E. OWEN.

DARLASTON'S INDEBTEDNESS TO AN ENTE[RPRISING] CAPTAIN OF INDUSTRY.

WONDERFUL COMMERCIAL PROGRE[SS]

WITH the death of Mr. Alfred Ernest Owen, sole proprietor in the well-known firm of Rubery, Owen and Company, constructional engineers, the South Stafford-shire district has lost one of its most enter-prising business men and Darlaston a citizen of sterling worth.

Although Mr. Owen stuck to his post as the head of the firm, it was known that for some time he had been ailing. Following an opera-tion five or six years ago, his condition improved, but in November he had to be taken to a Sutton Coldfield nursing home, where he died on Monday night from a stomach affection in his 51st year.

During the Christmas holidays he was sufficiently well to see several of the officials of his firm and was greatly cheered by the numerous flowers and good wishes re-ceived from employees in all departments of the works. These helped considerably to brighten his closing days.

On the last occasion that Mr. Owen addressed his workpeople—at the annual dinner of their bowling club on Saturday, November 23—he spoke of the great value of health compared with wealth. On the following Monday he was taken ill.

As recently as July last Mr. Owen paid [ra]tes, chiefl[y]

hasn't." Yet he was alwa[ys cour]teous. He despised the [slap]-pers progress. Mr. Owe[n prided him]-self on being an orator. [He had the] knack of getting to the [point] and his sincerity wo[n general] esteem.

Fittingly described a[s] Mr. Owen attached grea[t importance to] welfare and social side of industrial [life. He] built a spacious canteen and recreation grounds adjoining the works, and as far back as January, 1912, was one of the pioneers of the industrial welfare movement in the dis-trict. His efforts were then referred to in a London newspaper as "an oasis in a desert."

While lying ill he asked his eldest son to visit various old people in Darlaston at Christmas to ensure that they did not want, while in accordance with custom Mr. W. Hill (welfare superintendent), on his behalf, dis-tributed good things to the sick and deserv-ing among employees and their relatives. On the Saturday prior to Christmas 500 children [were] entertained at the canteen.

THE LATE MR. OWEN.

WORKERS' TRIBUTE.—A scene at the funeral of Mr. A. E. Owen at Sutton Coldfield on Saturday. Some 1,500 employees of Messrs. Rubery, Owen and Co., of Darlaston, were present.

Birmingham Gazette Jan 6th 1930.

A BELOVED EMPLOYER.

Hundreds of Workpeople at Councillor Owen's Funeral.

A Touching Tribute.

Large crowds were present at Sutton Cold-field Parish Church, on Saturday, when the late Councillor A. E. Owen was laid to rest. Councillor Owen, who was principal of the firm of Rubery, Owen and Co., of Darlaston, lived at New Hall, Sutton Coldfield, and was very highly respected in the town, where he was a prominent church worker.

37

1930-1945

On 26 July 1930 at the eighth annual sports day of the Victoria Club. Mrs F.L. Owen (holding the cup), accompanied on her right by her daughter Miss Jean Owen, presented the prizes to the winners of the various events. A.G.B. Owen standing next to his sister had taken over the management of the company with his brother E.W.B. Owen earlier in the year following the death of their father.

The Memorial Garden

On Saturday 7th May 1932 Mrs F.L. Owen opened The A.E. Owen Memorial Garden, which was close to the High Street, Darlaston. The area was laid out at the family's expense with the Council responsible for the garden's future maintenance.
The plaque (shown below) was later removed and relocated to the main entrance of Emmanuel Church, Bentley.

Pear Tree House, the imposing detached house in the background was built in 1852 for Edwin Bruerton a wealthy pawnbroker and property owner. Locals nicknamed it the 'Lion House' due to the cast iron lions that once adorned its gateposts.
Walsall Council has restored the Garden so it is once more a haven for those seeking peace and quiet after visiting the local shops and the supermarket (ASDA).

Taken on the 15th September 1934 before a 'Staff and Families
outing', the Dennis buses are outside the main offices in Booth Street.

**The following group of photographs all taken in the 1920s and 1930s illustrate
the Company's progress particularly that of the Structural Department.**

The West Stand under construction at Twickenham, Rugby Union's headquarters.
All of the steelwork was fabricated and erected by Rubery Owen.

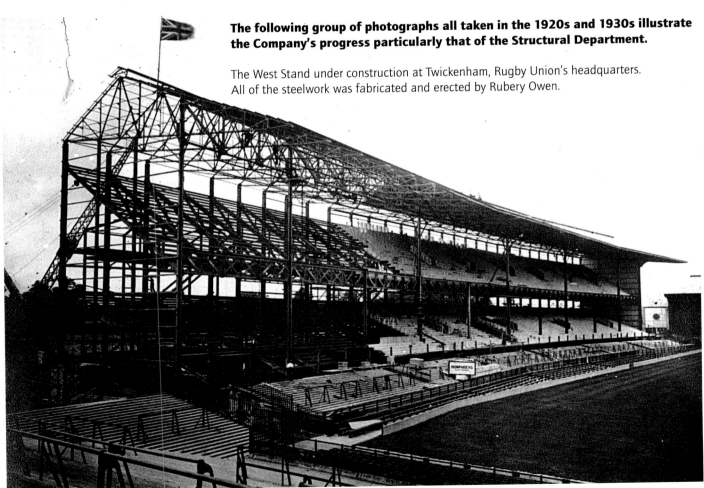

Stands for famous football clubs were also landmarks in the Company's history. This is the new Grand Stand for Manchester United.

Closer to home this stand was at Wolverhampton Wanderers.
Those interested in local history will recognise the Molineux hotel in the background.

Exports also began to grow. This footbridge under trial assembly in the Structural Department is destined for South African Railways.

Another Wolverhampton location, this time the new Welding Shop for The Chillington Tool Company.

The first consignment of girders leaving Darlaston for the railway bridge (L.&.N.E. line) over the Woodford Spur Road, London. The main girders were approx.17 tons each. A grand total of 220 tons of steelwork!

The close links with The Wellman Smith Owen Engineering Corporation continued. Here their 'Erecting Shop' in Darlaston is being constructed.

A 750 ton Metal Mixer designed by Wellman Smith Owen Corp. and manufactured by R.O.

An iron hopper boat, built for The Birmingham Canal Navigations, leaving the R.O. works entrance in Queen Street.
An unusual sight which already appears to have attracted local attention.

A certificate issued by R.O. to employees who had completed a course of Anti Gas Training. November 1938.

Signs being put up to indicate the location of the Air Raid Shelters for the Manufacturing Departments. Among the group Mr Staite is identified, (tall front centre).

Works Fireman, Arthur Birt, demonstrating the use of a bomb scoop. One method of dealing with the incendiary bombs that were dropped on the factory.

Aircraft assembly of Lancaster and Stirling bombers took place in the Air Frame Department 19. The photograph was taken in July 1941

We believe this mobile Salvation Army canteen was purchased from donations by R.O. employees. Celebrating the event and a good cuppa are A.G.B. Owen, E.W.B. Owen, G. Buckley, C. Partridge, W. Hunt, A. Gilbert, R. Hammond and W.J.W. Shelton.

An extract from the wartime recollections of Molly Williams (Gilbert) who with her sister Betty had their first jobs as typists with the Company just before and during the war period.

RECOLLECTIONS OF WORLD WAR 2
By
Molly Williams (Gilbert)

I was born in Darlaston and following are my recollections of the 1939-1945 war:-

Most people refused to believe there would be another war. There were too many terrible memories recalled by the older generation of the 1914-1918 war when thousands of men and boys never returned. It was also feared that the next time poison gas would be used, not only in the war zones but on civilians.

In 1938 Neville Chamberlain came back from Germany jubilant in the belief that he had averted war. However, the following twelve months gave us a breathing space to prepare for what became World War 2 when Germany invaded Poland, and on September 3rd 1939 the BBC announced that this Country was at war with Germany.

All 20 year old men were called up for Military service. A few whose work was essential to the war effort, in Engineering, etc., were kept back. Various Civil Defence organisations were speedily arranged. Many Ex-service men from World War one became the Local Defence Volunteers (LDV), later the Home Guard, who to begin with had to practice their 'Arms' drill with broomsticks! An Auxiliary Fire Service (AFS) which later became part of the National Fire Service was trained and most factories had their own fire brigades. More people joined the Ambulance services. Eventually everyone from aged 18 to late mid-age was obliged to do some form of Civil Defence unless they were too infirm or caring for very young children.

My sister Betty and I were in our first jobs as typists at Rubery Owen and Co. Each office had an Air-raid warden whose job was to ensure every person was ushered into a shelter in case of a raid. Office staff were spared for an hour or two to assemble civilian gas masks in the Canteen. These were packed in little cardboard boxes and were carried with a string "shoulder-strap". As time went on we could buy little shaped bags specially made to carry them in. As quickly as possible the whole population was supplied with gas masks and Identity Cards. (My I.D. number was CRNM 223-4). I still have the card.

Anderson air raid shelters were issued to each family. These were made from curved sheets of corrugated iron bolted together,

Continued/

The first batch of ammunition boxes leaving the factory, 11th August 1940.

Taken later in August 1940 a Bofors Gun carriage ready for dispatch.

The R.O. Home Guard Brass Band outside the canteen. The walls had been painted in wartime camouflage. Included in the group are Frank Jellyman, Frank Spittle, Arthur Mills and Lt. Col. Jack Page.

The Good Friday Service in 1942. Conducted by the Right Rev. Edward Woods, the Bishop of Lichfield. This was the first time he addressed the employees, this event was in the partially constructed Heavy Axle Case Department.

The Brass Band at the Good Friday Service. The band appears to be making its way through the factory.

The Bishop gave pride of place to his Darlaston visit for the Company's Good Friday Service for the next ten consecutive years. He described himself as the firm's 'Padre' and was fondly referred to by the workforce as the Good Friday Bishop of Industry.

Opposite page – top
To the order of the Ministry of Supply this picture shows the first operation in the making of a steel helmet shaped out of a square sheet. Many thousands were made throughout the war.

Opposite page – bottom
Waiting for the girls at the bench to fit the internal parts.

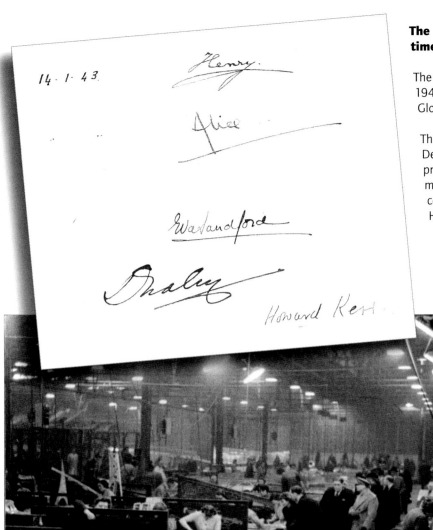

14.1.43.

Henry.

Alice

Wadandford

Howard Kerr

The Duke and Duchess of Gloucester made a war time visit

The Company's Visitors Book for the 14th January 1943. The entry being for the Duke and Duchess of Gloucester's party.

The Gloucesters started their tour in the Air Frame Department 19, where they viewed a range of wartime products. These included the manufacture of sea mine cases, bomb cases, aeroplane wings, aircraft components, armoured car bodies, Bofors guns and Howitzers including their allied munitions.

Air Frame Department 19

R.O.s St. John's Ambulance Brigade Nursing Staff, Security and the Fire Service. Mr. Essam in charge of the Works Police stands in the front row.

A.G.B. Owen initially greeted the Royal Party as Chairman of the Company on the Willenhall side of the factory. However, half-way through the tour, as they stepped over the border into Darlaston, A.G.B.O. had his chain of office put on as Chairman of Darlaston Urban District Council, and welcomed the party again, this time on behalf of the Council.

The Duke and Mr E.W.B. Owen chat with staff and Departmental personnel outside the entrance to the Armour Plate Department.

A range of weapons displayed for the benefit of the Royal Party.

The Duke inspects members of the 37th (Darlaston) Home Guard Battalion outside the R.O. Drill Hall in Queen St. Commanded by Lt. Col. Jack Page (in doorway). The royal family member is escorted round by Albert 'Nobby' Clarke who was to attain the rank of Major by the end of the Second World War.

A visit to the Day Nursery where employees could leave their children during working hours to be looked after by the Matron, Hilda Tilley and her staff.

Final goodbyes after an inspiring visit.

Sports Days at R.O.

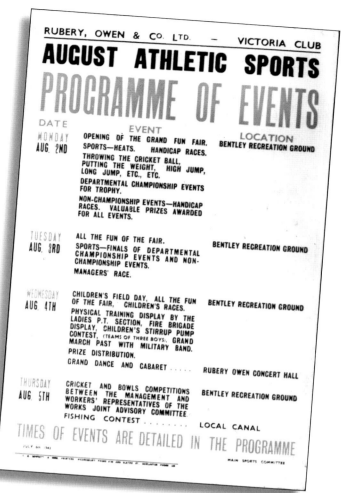

Advertising the programme of events put on by R.O. as part of Darlaston's 'Holiday at Home Scheme'.

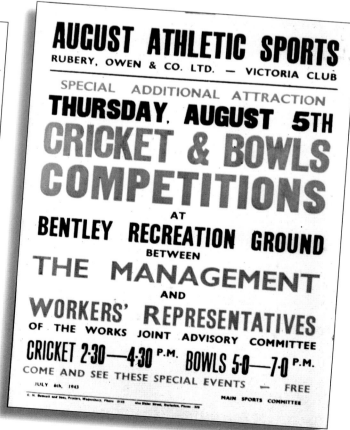

"WHAT'S WHAT"

GRAND
ATHLETIC SPORTS

August 2nd to August 5th, 1943

Souvenir Programme
RUBERY, OWEN & CO. LTD. — VICTORIA CLUB

RUBERY, OWEN & CO., LTD.   DARLASTON

VICTORIA SPORTS CLUB
President A. G. B. OWEN, Esq., J.P.

Athletic Sports
1943

MONDAY AND TUESDAY, AUGUST 2nd and 3rd,
HELD ON THE SPORTS GROUND, BENTLEY.

The Sports will be opened each day at 2-0 p.m.
Entrance free to all employees and relatives.

Spectators are asked to assist the Officials by keeping behind the barriers
Any infringement of this rule will cause great inconvenience and delay the
Programme.

KEY INDEX TO DEPARTMENTS.

AP Armour Plate.   SE Steel Equipment
Av Aviation   Str Structural
EE Electrical and Engineering   11 Dept. 11
Man Management   18 A.C. 18
MW Motor Wheel   19 A.F. 19

RULES.

(1) Competitors must report to the Stewards at the Competitors tent at
least five minutes before the race is run
All running arrangements will be made at the tents

(2) Competitors who are not present when the event is started will forfeit the
right to compete.

(3) The Sports Committee:
(a) Reserves the right to reduce or withhold the prizes for any event
in case of insufficient entries.
(b) Will not be responsible for any accidents happening on the ground
(c) Will not be responsible for lost property

C. H. Bowcott & Sons, Printers, Wednesbury and Darlaston.

The souvenir programme giving an index to the Departments involved and details of the rules.

G.B. Taylor of A.C.18 Department on his last lap before winning the 1 mile handicap race.

Competitors prepare for the Sack Race for Girls in the 'mixed' events category.

The Tug-of-War championship. The final involved Structural Department and Motor Frame, here being urged on by their respective coaches.

The Chairman of the Victoria Club, as Master of Ceremonies, Mr E.W. Hancock broadcast the events throughout the entire proceedings.

Everything stops for tea. The M.C. clearly showing he supported the 'Beverage' Plan.

Anyone for the Donkey Derby? The rides on Children's Field Day proved ,as always, very popular.

For this young lady, however, the outlook on the slide looks a little more uncertain. Despite encouragement from front and rear it all appeared a little too much to take.

Punch and Judy Show.

The next Owen generation watches and waits. Mrs F.L. Owen with her grandson David. His brother John is on the knee of Mrs A.G.B. Owen.

The Children's Bottle party.

The A.C. 18 team winners of the Inter Departmental Athletic Sports Challenge Cup. Included in the group are Jack Rainsbury, Vic Watson and G.B. Taylor.

While taking part in many of the events himself Mr. A.G.B. Owen as President of the Sports Club appears to be weighing up the odds for success.

On the 26th September 1943 "Battle of Britain Sunday" the Bishop of Lichfield, dedicated the Lych Gate at Saint Lawrence Church, Darlaston in memory of Councillor A.E. Owen. The monies had been raised by public subscription and the seats that went with it were in memory of George Harry Buckley who for many years had worked alongside A.E. Owen as a Director and Secretary of the Company.

MINISTRY OF AIRCRAFT PRODUCTION

MILLBANK.

S.W.1.

28th February, 1944.

Dear Mr. Owen,

I was much interested in my visit to Rubery Owens on Saturday. You are making a great variety of products and dealing with the problems thus raised with a skill and punctuality which has earned the gratitude of my Department. I was very glad to have the opportunity of talking to the workers and also of seeing your Joint Production Committee.

Lady Cripps joins me in thanking all those who welcomed us so kindly.

Yours sincere

A.G.B. Owen, Esq.,
Rubery Owen & Co. Ltd.,
Darlaston,

N/L

A letter from Sir Stafford Cripps in recognition of his visit.

E.W.B. Owen, W. Hill, E. Jones and C. Partridge are meeting Sir Stafford Cripps, Minister of Aircraft Production, in 1944, R.O.s 50th Jubilee Year.

Brigadier P.J. Slater D.F.C. welcomes 'Old Mother Riley' alias Mr W. 'Snowie' Elwell, as part of Darlaston's Wartime National Savings 'Salute the Soldier' campaign held June 3rd to 10th 1944.

Darlaston Scouts follow their Scoutmaster, Mr. Burns, while they file past the saluting platform located in Church St. Darlaston.

Probably the W.V.S. Ladies taking their turn to march past the Brigadier. One can only ponder how many of the participants and bystanders ended up at The Green Dragon Hotel.

A further selection of wartime products commencing with a depth charge thrower for the Navy.

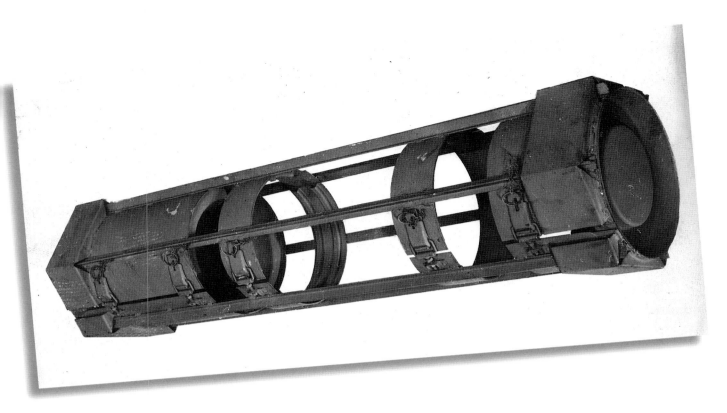

A special crate designed for the transit of bombs.

A 4-way Rotol Propeller hub before and during machining.

Sea Mine bases,
the two halves later
being joined to form
the more familiar
round shape.

Lorry leaving Darlaston loaded with chassis
frames towards the end of the war.

Even though the nearest sea was over a hundred miles away R.O. produced all-welded lifeboats.

The Rubery Owen chemistry laboratory.
F. Stokes is on the right facing the camera.

Mr & Mrs D. Hopkins the first host and hostess of 'Cadwgan', the Rubery Owen Group Convalescent home. The house was opened on the 25th September 1946, in the coastal village of Dyffryn Ardudwy, North Wales.

At Trade Fairs, R.O. Darlaston displayed their products under the umbrella of the Owen Organisation

The Owen Organisation Stand at the British Industries Fair, Castle Bromwich, Birmingham 6th May 1947.

Easiclene displayed their full range of domestic products.

Apprentices

The Apprentice Training School was opened on October 24th 1947 by Paymaster General H.A. Marquand. M.P.

The Apprentices watched the proceedings.

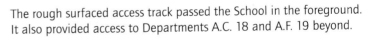

The rough surfaced access track passed the School in the foreground.
It also provided access to Departments A.C. 18 and A.F. 19 beyond.

A John Shaw press being operated in the Motor Frame Hot Press Department.

Gala Day 4th September 1948. The Ladies 'Slow' Cycle race is in progress.

The Inter-Works Championship half mile race, won by H. Buckley of R.O. Darlaston with F. Main of Electro-Hydraulics second.

Sons of Rest

August 1949. The Joint Managing Directors with employees and the Chairman of the Darlaston Urban District Council, Mr. Harmer Nicholls, at the opening of the Sons of Rest Workshop. It was started for employees retiring from the shop floor. The workshop enabled the men to continue light work and it also supplied the company with much needed small and awkward parts.

A contented group of S.O.R. men at work, all of them aged over seventy years.

The same group relaxing at their 'break-time'.

A staged photograph taken in the works to promote Industrial Safety Awareness. "Whispering Willie" was part of the firm's propaganda campaign.

David H. Griffiths who served the company for 57 years retired from the S.O.R. Workshop in 1971. Here he is promoting the saving of National Savings Certificates in the late 1940s.

Precision aircraft parts and Bright bolts and nuts produced at the Darlaston Factory.

Building chassis frames in the large assembly shops.

Christmas parties 1952

Held on the top floor of the canteen, the children's Christmas parties were one of the highlights of the year. December 13th 1952.

Parents and grandparents wait in the lower canteen.

Coronation 2nd June 1953

To celebrate the 1953 Coronation, the offices in Booth Street, were decorated and floodlit.

Works Trip to London for the Coronation. Part of a convoy of eighteen coaches.

Coronation Queen
Miss June Hanwell
centre with her
attendants Miss
Betty Farmer on
the left and
Miss Dorothy
Shelley.

The Old People's Coronation Party 18th June.

Apprentices

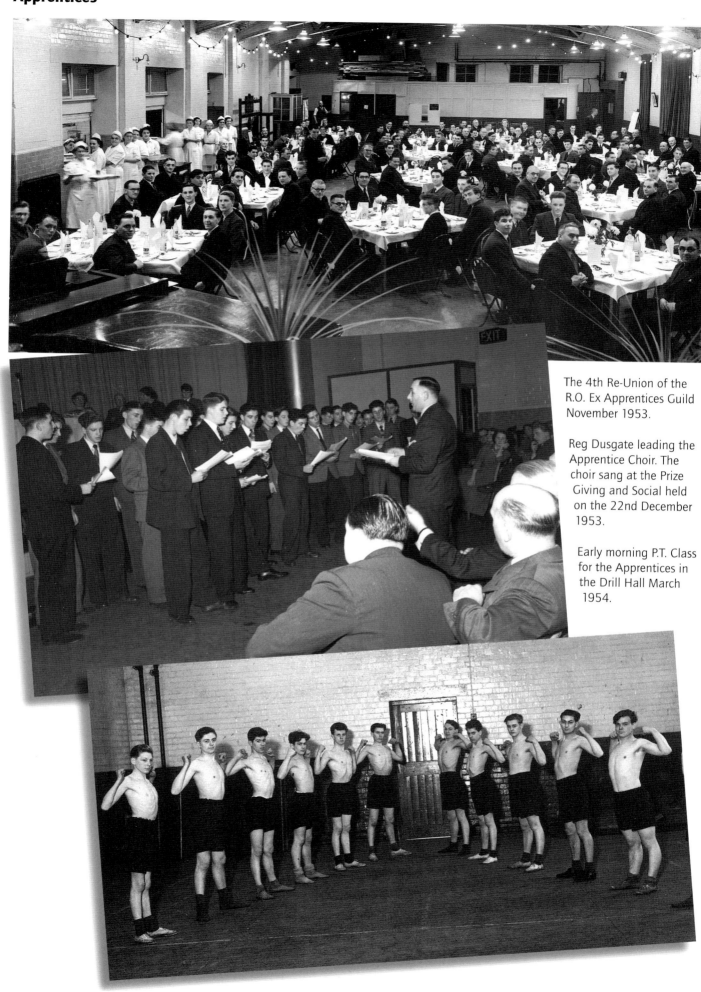

The 4th Re-Union of the R.O. Ex Apprentices Guild November 1953.

Reg Dusgate leading the Apprentice Choir. The choir sang at the Prize Giving and Social held on the 22nd December 1953.

Early morning P.T. Class for the Apprentices in the Drill Hall March 1954.

Pantomime and Drama Clubs

The entire cast in a scene from the R.O. Drama Club's 1954 production of 'Blithe Spirit' held in May. *Front, left to right:* Vi Futty, Dennis Doolley, Eve Burrell.
Behind: Ron Harbridge, Margaret Jackson, Anne Bullock and Betty Wilkinson.

'Babes in the Wood' produced by the R.O. Pantomime Club 1955.
It attracted record attendances running from January 24th to February 5th.
Left to right, C. Pinson, C. Staite, B. Jones, B. Smy, G. Davies. *Sitting*: B. Smy and M. Whitehouse.

R.O. 2nd Eleven Cricket Team 1954
Back: R. Nicholson, K. Ross, C. Morgan, T. Butler, A. Moreton, J. Butler, A. Summerhill, Umpire F. Stead.
Front: W. Steadhouse, J. Rumble (Vice.C) H. Gay, S. Crutchley (C) and scorer C. Crutchley.

Archery Team 1954
Left: Mrs Taylor, C. Harris, A.B. Taylor and N. James.

Sports Day
10th July 1954

The winning Tug-of-War team Motor Frame 'A' making a last strenuous effort to win the cup.

Smith of R.O. Darlaston winning the Inter-works Championship half mile with R.O. Wrexham in 2nd place.

This amusing skit on the end of meat rationing earned the Entertainments Section fourth prize with their 'Free at Last' tableau.

The Hockey Team

Back: A. Boyce, H. Guest, F. Beddows (C.) G. Smith, R. Russell, B. Cooney, J. Russell.
Front: R. Moorehouse, R. Hawthorne, H. Lloyd, E. Smith, W. Lawrence.

Members of the R.O. Photographic Club held a Portraiture Evening on November 10th. Mr P. Tyler (Vice President) *extreme left,* gave a talk on the subject. Four attractive girls from R.O. volunteered to let members try and put his remarks into practice, on the understanding that they wished to remain anonymous and no telephone numbers were to be given out!.

The new "Rubery Owen" Division of the St. John's Ambulance Brigade registered in June 1953 replaced the previous one. In their first year these volunteers provided over 400 hours of duty at various R.O. functions and dealt with 47 casualties

Nine Midland firms took part in a Civil Defence Exercise on October 28th at B.S.A.'s Sports Ground, Small Heath, Birmingham. R.O. provided the staff for the casualty clearing station and a full rescue team.

Christmas Parties
These volunteers assisted on two Saturdays prior to Christmas to organise five children's parties.

3000 children of employees would have attended.

Work in progress on a large chassis in the Motor Frame Department for the Birmingham and Midland Motor Omnibus Co. The chassis was for the double-decker Midland 'Red'.

Three generations of Owens at the annual horticultural show. Florence Owen on the right, Mrs Jean Stanley, a Director of the company and sister of A.G.B. and E.W.B. Owen, with her four children, Thomas, Caroline, Bobbie and Edward. Mrs Patricia Owen, wife of E.W.B. Owen with her son Charles, is behind.

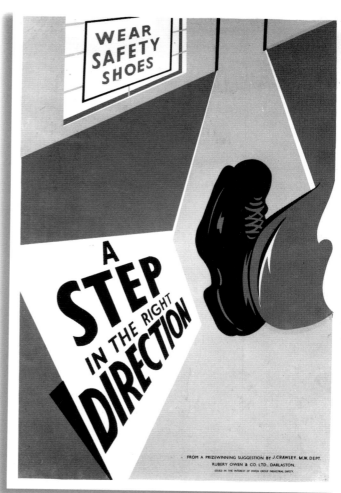

Safety

Prize winning posters for promoting safety which were to be displayed round the factory.

The last Safety Meeting under the Chairmanship of Mr H.S. Price organised a special exhibition of Progress in Safety. It was opened by A.G.B. Owen with H.S. Price, W.L. Hurdman, (the new Chair), and E.W.B. Owen.

R.O. Fire Brigade

The ground by the nearby canal provided an excellent training site for the R.O. Fire Fighters.

The men of the R.O. Fire Brigade stand with their equipment outside the Works Fire Station.

Gala day July 9th 1955

Department 15, strong supporters of Walsall F.C. named their float 'Mid Summer Nights Dream'. The Dept. won third prize.

Aviation's Pirate Ship "Black Hawk" crowded with bold buccaneers was First.

The children's and family events were enjoyed by competitors and spectators alike, the effort to be first to the tape is clearly seen.

George Bailey, extreme left, came second in his Fancy Dress as an Indian Salesman.
There was a children's prize as well.

The Welfare Office at R.O.
Dealing with the paying out of sickness benefits.

On August 8th Zoe Newton of Milk Publicity fame came to Darlaston to promote fresh milk in the works and canteen. She visited the Children's Nursery as part of her tour.

'What's My Line?'

Gilbert Harding, a member of the above T.V. panel game, appears to be quite domesticated washing up at an R.O. Easiclene sink unit at the Scottish Ideal Home Exhibition.

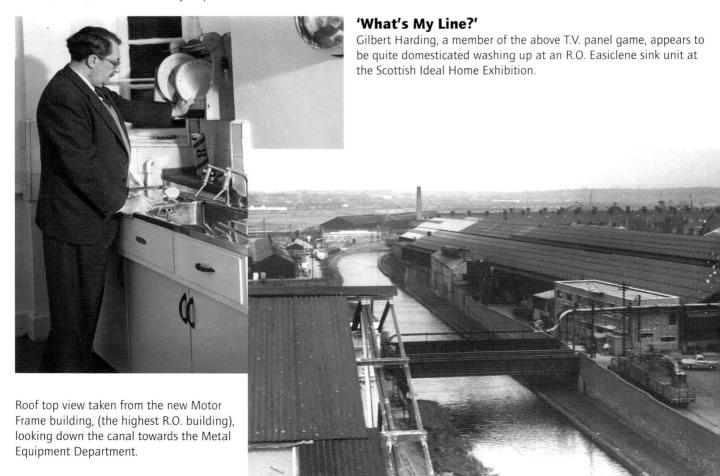

Roof top view taken from the new Motor Frame building, (the highest R.O. building), looking down the canal towards the Metal Equipment Department.

Grace Owen opened the Annual Arts and Crafts and Chrysanthemum Show in October 1955.

Grace Owen presenting the A.E. Statham Photographic Trophy to Stan Griffiths at the annual prize giving.

On November 3rd The Queen accompanied by the Duke of Edinburgh opened the Colleges of Technology, Commerce and Art in the centre of Birmingham. R.O. had a particular pride in the building having provided and erected over 3000 tons of structural steelwork fabricated in the Darlaston Shops. Over six hundred detailed shop drawings were made.

Christmas Parties 1955

The tired young man on the right at the annual Christmas party appears to have finished his jelly and is busy falling asleep over his drink.

The wonder of Christmas is expressed in the faces of these rather shy young ladies having just received their presents from the two 'joint' Father Christmases.

A record number of Christmas presents were distributed to employees' families. Two members of the Welfare Department are about to embark on the mammoth task of wrapping them.

A new R.O. Rugby Club was formed by the Apprentices in 1955. Team for the first match was:-
Back row: C. Roberts, M. Farley, L. Turner, A. Hill, A. Fletcher, J. Brown, G. Wilkins, G. Williams.
Front row: G. Owens, W. Myatt, E. Edwards, B. Logan, T. Myring, M. Dorricott, J. Thorne.

The 3000 ton British Clearing Press was up and working in the new department of Motor Frame in January 1956. At the time it was the largest of its type in the country.

Prebendary S. Linsley conducted the 30th March 1956 service when everyone joined in the singing of the Good Friday favourite hymn 'There is a green hill...".

A record in civic work. *Left,* Mayor of Wednesbury Councillor J.E. James (Motor Frame), *centre*, A.G.B. Owen, Chairman of Staffordshire C.C. and *right*, Chairman of Darlaston Urban D.C. Councillor Wilf Partridge (Engineering). All three being employees of R.O. Darlaston.

On the 20th December 1956 a total of 364 prizes were given out to the Engineering and Commercial Students including 36 girls. June Finch in the light dress standing next to A.G.B. Owen still works part-time for the company.

The January 1957 panto club production of 'Bluebeard' starred Bill Smy in the title role and Margaret Foster as principal girl 'Fatima' with her father 'Count Ten' Ginger Boyd. The cast pictured with the Bette Guest troupe of girls.

The 1956-57 season was another successful one for the R.O. Netball team.
Left, D. Groves, J. Tandy, F. Coulton, L. Whitehouse, P. Stone (C.), M. Law, M. Cooksey and J. Latham.

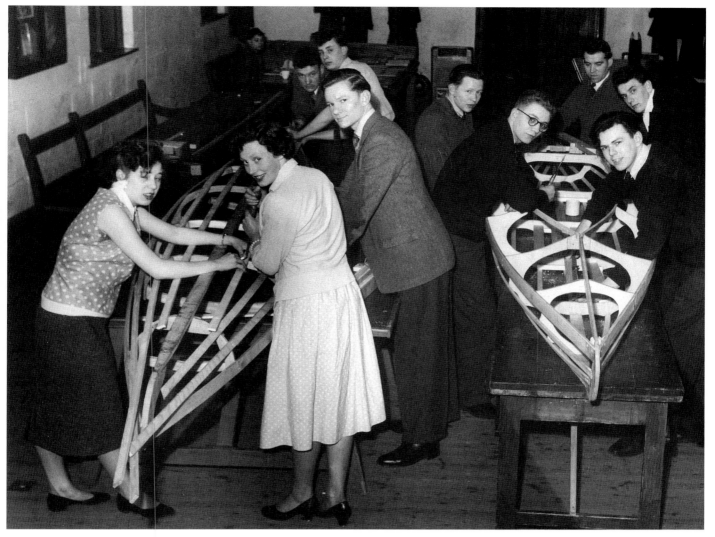

After a suggestion that the R.O. Youth Club might like to tackle something constructive, this enterprising group, including Sally Talbot, Margaret Cooksey, Brian Griffiths, Alan Stanton, John Shaw, Glyn Owens, David Carr, Michael Ralph, with no previous 'D.I.Y' experience, started from scratch on the construction of canoes. The result proved surprisingly professional.

On Easter Saturday the First and Second R.O.D. Football teams took on their counterparts from R.O. Warrington. Honours were about even, the 1st team won 6-1 and 2nd team lost 5-1.

Gala Day 1957

The pouring rain failed to dampen the spirits of the day although the date 13th July may have had something to do with it. The nursery rhyme float won 2nd prize for Armour Plate Dept.

We believe this features one of the Apprentice Sports Final events.

During 1957 a new apprentice in the form of a Ruston Hornsby diesel joined the other works locos. Certainly quieter and cleaner than its predecessors, but for the more loco minded, the newcomer did not have quite the same attraction.

In October the Contracts Division celebrated the Completion of the 1000th Drott Skid Shovel.

A. Arnold, C. Peplow, J. Cooke, B. Wells, J. Staite, E.W.B. Owen, E. Dudley, J.T. Plumley, W. Hartshorne, T.R.S. Lloyd, A. Cox, J. Holder, J. Henden, K. Williams, C. Turner, H. Hince, H. Allen, F. Morran.

Two 81 ft. long girders (to build a canal bridge) travelled through the narrow streets of the Bullstake area of Darlaston en route to a steel works at Brierley Hill on 27th February. The journey caused some excitement and dislocation of traffic but was happily completed without serious mishap.

On February 10th and 11th 1958 the local Old Age Pensioners were able to attend a revue called 'Gaytime' put on by the R.O. Concert Party, in place of the normal Christmas panto. The dancers from the Mavis Smith School assisted, earning great applause from the appreciative audience.

At the Long Service Awards Dinner held in July 1957, A.G.B. and E.W.B. Owen surprised their mother Mrs F.L. Owen by presenting her with a Certificate for 57 years service. This was timely as she sadly died the following June.

The Horticultural Section of the R.O. Sports and Social Club in March were hosts for a recording of BBC's Gardeners' Question Time. The visiting experts were Fred Loads, Freddy Grisewood (C.), Alan Gemmell and Bill Sowerbutts.

At the Good Friday
Service Prebendary Linsley
spoke about personal
relationships in industry
ending the service with
the traditional laying of a
wreath of spring flowers
at the Company's War
Memorial.

'Workers' Playtime' was broadcast from R.O. Warrington on February 27th and R.O. Darlaston on May 15th 1958. The Artistes at Darlaston
welcomed by E.W.B. Owen and Tom Wilkinson included Richard Murdoch, Marion Keene, Paddy Edwards and Douglas Maynard.

The Inter-Departmental Angling Competition took place on June 21st over a stretch of water, the rights of which had recently been acquired by the Club, along the canal between Forsters Bridge and Barnes Meadow Bridge.

The Gala Day on July 12th was once more wet although the spirits of Joe Eaton, Vivian Andrew and Horace Allen (Contracts Div.) appear in no way dampened as they carried off 1st prize.

On 24th September A.G.B. Owen presented 23 of the Firm's drivers with awards in connection with the National Safe Driving Competition. Mrs J. Robinson receiving a Bar to her medal.

The 'back room boys' the garage mechanics.
Back: F. Kinder, K. Perry, E. Harper, C. Wassley, S. Brookes, G. Hayes, B. Aston.
Front: E. Woodall, R. Neale, C. Anderson, without their efficient maintenance there would have been no 'safe' drivers.

Another Rubery Owen Christmas tradition involved the handing over of Apple of Gold calendars as gifts to the Firm's pensioners.

Leabank displayed their full range of products at the 1958 Business Efficiency Exhibition at Manchester including the daring 'modern' colours of orange and cream.

BLISS PRESS

Automation comes to Axle Case Dept. R.O. Darlaston

PART I

...ing with their inherent interest ...ering progress, allied to an ... demand for the particular ... Darlaston have embarked ...lete modernisation of the ...he manufacture of heavy

...nt has only been ...operation of some of ...o constitute the ...heavy commercial ...heir agreeing to ...ign of rear axle ...able for mass

...nufacturing ...t that at ...vy axle ...month ...tal of

...e- ...y

Automation came to the Axle Case Department (C.1959) when the Bliss Press was modified. This rear view of the Press shows the powered track leading to the cooling towers.

On January 30th 1959 the Labour M.P. for Wednesbury, Mr John Stonehouse, had lunch after his party speech in the Works Canteen. He is sitting on the right next to Doug Peach (Work's Convenor) in the company of Harold Smith (Shop Steward).

Mr Rollinson and Mr Haynes can be named from among this happy group of R.O. roofers all members of the Engineering Department. It is thought their smiles might have something to do with the fact they had just received their 'Safety Award Bonus'.

Horace Meadows with his manager R.W. Latham receives a Good Housekeeping Certificate as Safety Representative for Section 11 of the Light Axle Main Shop. Other members of the Safety Committee watch.

Delegates at the inaugural Preparation for Retirement Conference in the picturesque grounds of Brandon Hall, May 1959

'Project '59'. Terry Myring (apprentice) is welcomed back from a Continental trek by members of the organising panel.

Motor Wheel Department, (circa 1960) a hive of industry with wheels travelling down track lines during their manufacture.

The Bentley Sports Ground probably in 1950s. One can only guess what Charlie Pinson might be saying to his R.O. Fire Brigade colleague while they demonstrate their fire drill skills.

The R.O. Cricket Team (circa 1960)

Back: Umpire (Unknown), R. Mitra, C. Wood, V. Jeavons, V. Peace, V. Unitt, E. Heaven.
Front: (Unknown), (Unknown), H. Willey (C), C.Myring, F. Hughes.
Front: V. Unitt (Jnr.) Scorer.

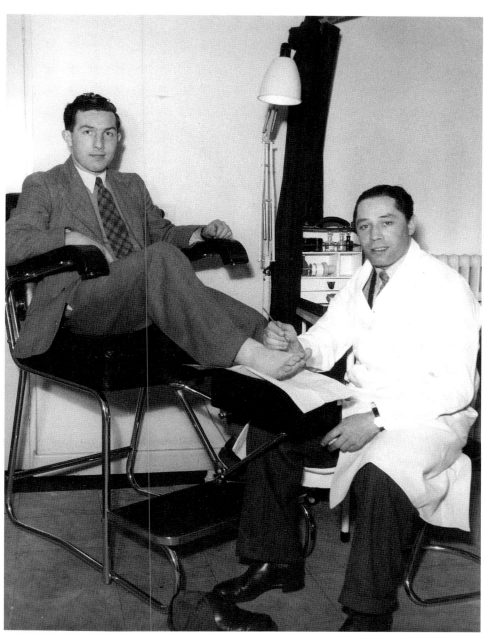

We could not resist the temptation of including this photograph of Stan Jeavons treating Billy Crook during one of his chiropody sessions. In 1949 Billy a draughtsman in R.O.s Structural Department played right half for the victorious Wolves team in the F.A. Cup.

Mrs Coupland presented prizes at the 1960 Fire Brigade Tournament.

Mrs Jean Stanley, (a Director of the company), opened the Annual Arts and Crafts and Chrysanthemum Exhibition in October 1960. She received a bouquet from Miss M. Saunders, Sec Arts and Crafts Section and Arthur Webb, Chair of the Horticultural Society.

The Research and Development Department always prided themselves that their gala float would be topical and full of innovation. Recognised in the winning group are P. Spear, G. Baldwin, R. Hankinson, J. Bosworth and R. Neville.

R.O. Drama Club's 1960 production of the comedy 'Sailor Beware'. The cast: Doris Turpin, Joyce Dennis, Judy Latham, George Taylor, Peter Hollingshead, Trevor Hind, Beryl van-de-Hoek, Joan Startin and Brian Steen.

In June 1960 an idea was finally realised with the first Dinner of the newly formed Superintendents' and Foremen's Association. Included are J. Broome, T. Edwards, A. Foster, F. Unitt and B. Roberts.

1961 TO PRESENT

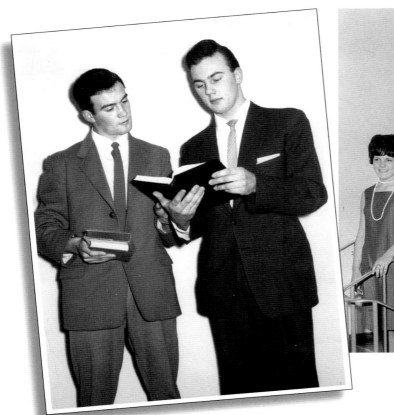

Contestants line up for the 1962 Miss Sunshine competition. The winner was Anne McGarrie with her attendants Jackie Watkins and Edna John.

The 12th Annual Prize Distribution, David Russell *(left)* and Ray Dunkley *(right)* winners of the P.J. Freeman and J.T. Page memorial prizes for the best all-round Engineering Apprentices. Ray Dunkley is now a Director of Rotech Laboratories.

Mr G. Roe presenting Mrs Price with a silver coffee set on her retirement from the R.O. Receiving Office.

February 1961, the first Owen Organisation Motoring Club (O.O.M.C.) Dinner/Dance at the Elms Hotel, Aldridge.
Club trophy winners B. Pickering, J. Shaw, N. Ferris and B. Patterson. On the far left is David Owen, General Manager of Motor Division.

Delegates at an Industrial Life Conference for R.O. Staff at Ashorne Hill, near Warwick. The leader was Rev. Bruce Reed, who represented a Christian approach to industry, designed to be of benefit to all employees. April 1961.

Bentley Hall Brick Co. Ltd. (part of the R.O. Group) was based less than a mile away from the Darlaston factory. Their bricks were used to build many of the houses in the area up to the Company's closure in the mid 70s. Here brick setters move cars of green bricks into the kiln for drying and burning.

The procession of witnesses going to the ceremony of the laying of the foundation stone for the new Emmanuel Church, 1954.

Jim Owen with his parents Mr A.G.B. Owen and Mrs Viva Owen at the consecration of Emmanuel Church, Saturday 21 July 1956.

Royal visit

Wednesday 21st November 1962 was a "Red Letter Day" in the annals of R.O. Darlaston when H.R.H. Princess Margaret and her husband the Earl of Snowdon visited the works.

Greeted by Sir Alfred who had met the Princess frequently due to their shared involvement with Dr. Barnado's Homes. The official welcome was by the Lord Lieutenant of the County, Mr. H. Wallace with R.O.s St. John's Ambulance Brigade providing a guard of honour.

The tour commenced with a visit to the Motor Wheel Department, followed by Frames and Assemblies, Bolt and Nut and the Contracts Divisions, then on to the Service Departments, Medical, Personnel and the Nursery. At every stage they showed a keen interest in the Company's products talking readily with the employees.

From every point of view 1962 was a happy year for Rubery Owen characterised by winning the Drivers' Championship for Graham Hill and the Constructors' Championship for the Company thanks to Graham and Richie Ginther's efforts in their B.R.M.'s. Here Sir Alfred in jubilant mood congratulates Graham Hill on winning the final Grand Prix in South Africa and the Championship.

The R.O. Group (including Darlaston) put all their resources behind the building of the 'Bluebird' car for Donald Campbell at Motor Panels, Coventry. After many delays and frustration he gained the land speed record of 403.1 m.p.h. on July 17th 1964 driving over the salt beds of Australia's Lake Eyre.

Donald Campbell (left) inspects the car with Jim Philips.

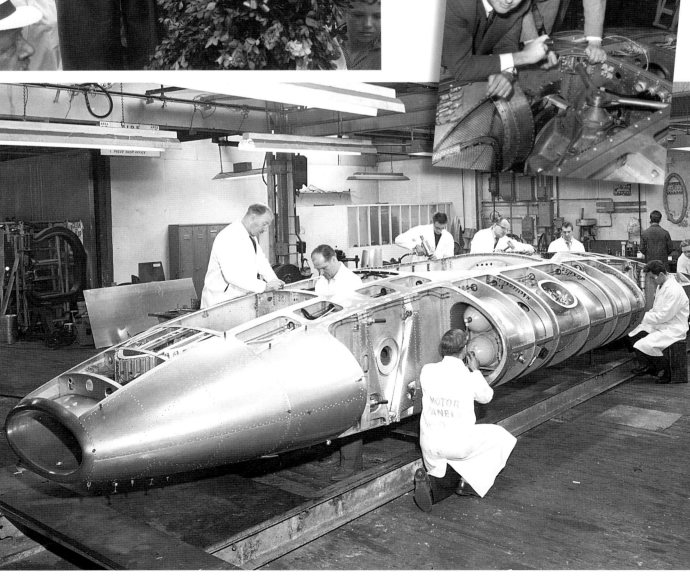

Chain making was one of the crafts associated with the Midlands. Chains Ltd. started in 1910 (with A.E. Owen) but from 1941 was based on the Holyhead Road, Moxley, Wednesbury. Here Mrs Lily Goodwin with 48 loyal years with the company, inspects for faults.

The Structural Division provided an 'umbrella' completed in just sixty-five hours over August bank holiday 1963. It carried intersecting traffic of Regent Street and Oxford Street. The ticket hall of the underground station could then be built underneath involving an additional 1,100 tons of steelwork.

Trip to London to 'see the sights', 1963

2000 R.O. employees and their families travelled to London to 'see the sights' for the Annual Works Outing.
Four trains stopped at 20 stations in the Black Country area. 200 employees also went in a fleet of coaches.

Many returned in the
small hours after seeing
the 'Black and White
Minstrel' show.

Sir George Eddy, Midland Regional member of the National Savings Committee congratulates Sir Alfred and his Committee, on reaching the £3 million mark in National Savings at the Darlaston works.

In March 1964 employees and local lorry drivers breathed a sigh of relief that finally the Owen Road, Willenhall, (that linked to the Midland Road, Darlaston) was to be tarmaced and to become a permanent thoroughfare. Local wags often referred to the potholes as 'no man's land'.

An Electric Welding Machine operated in Department 11 used for eye protection publicity by the Safety Office.

At the opening of the R.O. bowling greens at Bentley for the 1964 season, Sir Alfred was heard to remark after he was beaten 11 to 1 by his brother "I am sure he has had a bit of practice." Surely one of the great understatements of the year!

Gold wrist watches awarded in June 1964 in recognition of 50 years service with R.O. at Darlaston.
Left to right: Harold Heaven (MW), David Griffiths (FA), Bryce Cresswell (Bolt & Nut), Thomas Ryder (SOR), Harry E. Jones (SOR).
David Owen, General Manager of Motor Division, stands between A.G.B.O. and E.W.B.O. with Les Warner (Wks. Mgr. Aviation) and
John Dinwoodie (General Mgr. B & N Div) on the extreme right.

Fred Griffiths, in the centre, was presented with a suite of 'Leabank' furniture for his Wolverhampton Office when he took over as full time Secretary for the Wolverhampton district of the Amalgamated Engineering Union, relinquishing his position as R.O.s Works Convenor. The complimentary dinner in his honour at the Royal Hotel, Walsall was attended by more than a hundred people.

'Greenfingers' Arthur Webb at the Victoria Road allotments tells Elizabeth Owen and Frank Jellyman the secret of his giant leeks having won the premier award for the best R.O. Allotment for the 24th consecutive year.

The R.O. Fire Brigade at the Annual Gala Day.

Rumour has it that E.W.B. Owen was quick to ensure that this sign appeared 'Left for Arthur Webb'. The accident having taken place outside the Horticultural Store.

Arnold Worthy (Mgr Heavy Axle Case Dept) showing prominent Czechoslovakian Trade Officials round.
(Part of the policy of encouraging East/West Trade).

Fran Tennis, Chief Engineer *(Centre)* from Husco Valve (U.S.A.) inspecting a batch of Husco Valves made by R.O. with Ken Robinson Mgr. on the left and Frank Lee, Asst. Gen. Mgr. (Contracts Division), on the right.

R.O.s links with British Motor Corporation

Spring 1965. Five and a half years after its introduction, R.O. congratulated the British Motor Corporation when the millionth Mini came off the production lines in Birmingham.

Spot welding operations undertaken with a mini sub-frame nearing completion.

The Motor Wheel Department produced vast numbers of wheels from 10 to 20 inches diameter.

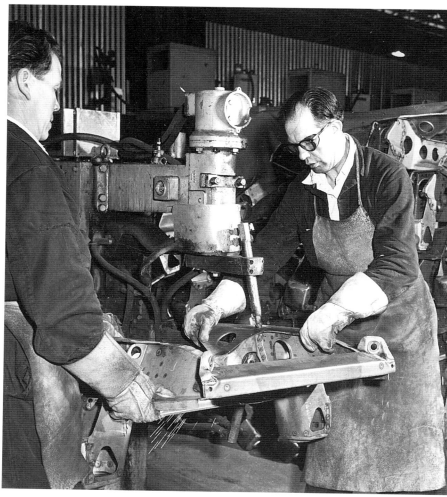

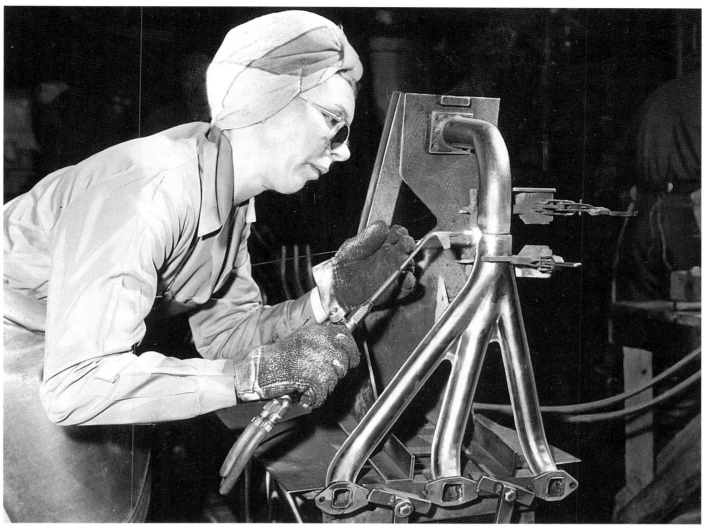

Final assembly of the exhaust manifold for the Mini Cooper 'S' type.

The Austin Mini Countryman (shown below) was similar to the Mini Saloon, but had a longer wheel base and a slightly stiffer rear suspension to cope with additional loads.

John Wilkinson (S.O.R.), standing beside E.W.B.O., with his china cabinet presented by Sir Alfred for 65 years service going back to 1900. John had every intention to continue to work in the industrial protective clothing section of the S.O.R. David Owen is in the centre with his fiancé, Ethne Sowman.

A gold plated hub from the B.R.M. that won the 1962 South African G.P. (driver Graham Hill) was presented to the departmental winners of the Quality and Reliability Campaign, (1964). Arnold Worthy accepts the Trophy for the Heavy Axle Case Department.

Jackie Stewart in his first year with B.R.M. at the British Grand Prix at Silverstone July 10th 1965.

The Rover B.R.M. gas turbine powered car (number 31) competed in the 24 hr race at Le Mans, 1965. (A joint venture between R.O. and Rover Co. Ltd). Graham Hill, complete with neck support, runs to his car at the start.

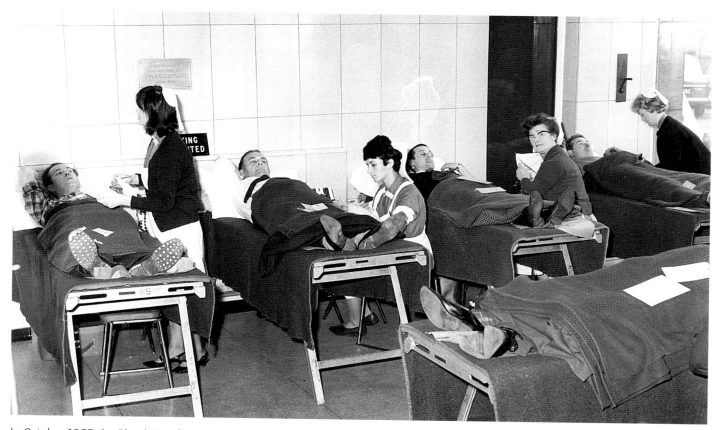

In October 1965 the Blood Transfusion Service made one of their regular visits to Darlaston.

Graham Hill and Jackie Stewart came first and second in their 2 litre B.R.M.s in New Zealand, January 1966. This was their first appearance in Australasia as part of the Tasman series of races and a real morale boost for the two Australian based engineering companies Rubery Owen & Kemsley Pty. Ltd. and Conveyancer Fork Lift Trucks (Australia) Pty. Ltd.

On the 5th February 1966, Ted Heath opened the King's Hill Works, which was part of a vast company expansion programme. During the proceedings the Work's black cat wished the company good luck.

Later, when Heath was Prime Minister, local wags wrote this.

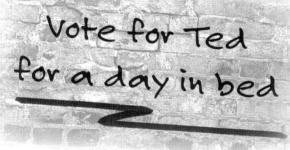

This ingenious display on productivity by the Heavy Axle Case Dept. echoed R.O.s management and employees aim to increase productivity by 10%. The R.O. Group of Companies planned to export £4.5 million worth of goods.

Probably the largest mechanical 4 tie bar press in the world (designed and built by Weingarten) came into production in 1966. (Making chassis side members). The 4000 ton capacity press weighed 960 tons with a bed size 12.8 metres long. Now R.O. had one of the most comprehensive Cold Press Shops in Europe with presses ranging from 250 up to 4000 tons.

Four members of a ten man Soviet trade mission visited British Motor and Motor Component Companies for a fact finding tour in 1967. They showed a particular interest in the production of heavy side members for commercial vehicles by the Weingarten press.

David Treen, Research Engineer carrying out tests on an axle beam, set up on the Fatigue Rig, in the R. and D. Dept.

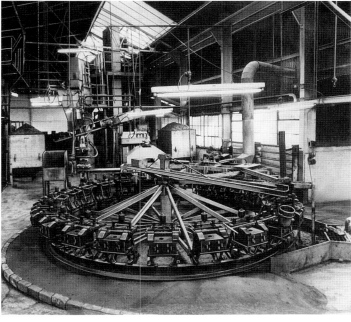

Directors of Platt Malleable Castings Ltd. visited the R.O. Stand at the Foundry Exhibition in Birmingham's Bingley Hall to place an order for their third Hallsworth moulding unit to be installed at their Walsall factory.

Introduced into the British market in 1967 a G.600 Gradall multi-purpose hydraulic excavator, an earthmoving machine of great versatility. Manufactured at the King's Hill factory in association with the Warner and Swasey Co. of Cleveland U.S.A.

Common sense prevailed with the signing of an Agreement, after straight discussions, between R.O. Management and Shop Stewards to avert their participation in the threatened engineering dispute October 1968.
Left to right: (Standing) A Sharratt (T & G.W.U. Sec.) J. Peake (T & G.W.U. Deputy Chairman) J.T. Pope (T & G.W.U. Deputy Convenor), R. Whiles (G & M.W.U, King's Hill Snr Shop Steward), H. Mountfield (E.T.U.), R. Rollason (A.E.F. King's Hill Snr Shop Steward), A. Onions (A.E.F. Convenor) J. Holland (A.E.F. Sec.). J. Robinson (A.E.F. Chairman) seated H. Smith (T. & G.W.U. Convenor) Sir Alfred Owen, Fred Straw (Director of Production Services).

In the presence of John and David Owen, Deputy Joint Managing Directors, their father Sir Alfred presented gold watches for 50 years service to J. Owen (no relation), *2nd left,* and W. Smy.

The Owen Karricon 304. A completely new straddle machine to handle and stack two high I.S.O transport containers in storage parks and marshalling yards. The 'Karricon' is shown handling another product from the same factory, part of a £1.5m container contract for Manchester Liners Ltd.

The Atlantic Steam Navigation Co. installed an 'Owen Travelift' to handle their container traffic at Felixstowe

The new giant the 'Karrilift 90' was first demonstrated at Darlaston. The Karrilift, larger and more powerful than its sister machines Travelift and Karricon, was designed to complement them rather than replace. All three were manufactured at King's Hill.

Works Security on Parade (circa 1971) *Back:* B. Jeffrey, W.H. Rudge, J. Pugh, A. Cotterill, A. Morris, J. Wright, R. Robinson.
Front: R. Foxall, G. Peake, Sgt. J. Somerfield, Security Chief Officer A. Botterill, Sgt. S. Foster, J. Brittle, A. Brazier.

Spring 1969. R.O. apprentices P. Ratcliffe, G.N. Butcher, F. Titley, T. Harrison, B. Cartwright, D. Bullers, J. Lewis, J. Mills, P. Birch, A. Kennard, R. Orme and A. Martin under the leadership of John Ruck and Michael Hogg took part in a leadership and initiative training expedition based at the Boys' Brigade Camp at Dyffryn. Joined by Bill Telling (Management Observer).

The 1972 intake of Apprentices and Graduates came up with the concept of the 'Romobile' following the philosophy 'If you want something the R.O. Group of Companies may well make it'. Components in its make up included the proverbial kitchen sink, a 4-in-1 bucket, a central heating radiator, an engine block, gas bottles, wheel hubs, commercial vehicle door panels, office chairs, an agricultural plough, topped off with a wheelbarrow for a roof.

Jean Owen standing next to her father on the opening of The Rhinog Holiday Estate.

At the end of the holiday season members of the R.O. Sixty Nine Club visited Dyffryn staying at the new Rhinog Chalets for a week-end as part of their social activities. Membership of the Club was open to anyone who had taken part in the Company's Preparation for Retirement Courses.

Mrs N. Bayliss trying out the Chairmobile mobile platform made by R.O. and invented by Lord Snowdon for the severely handicapped or for use during convalescence. It was a fitting tribute to her late husband, Norman Bayliss, who had first suggested it should be purchased following an Appeal to the Staff and Works Employees.

March 1974, Alan Stanway, Manager, presented a brass lantern to Derek Painter, on the eve of his wedding, on behalf of his friends in the R.O. Group Technical Services Dept.

The Library (Darlaston) was accessible to any employee. Linda Green dealt with correspondence, Valerie James (Librarian) checked British Standards from the filing cabinet and Judith Holt (Enquiry Officer) took calls.

An R.O. Wedding

Will Eaton of Financial Accounts Dept. Darlaston and Elaine Stoker, secretary to Bill Holmes (R.O. Holdings, Director), received a wedding gift from their friends in the Boardroom, on the occasion of their marriage. Elaine is still working for the Holding Company.

Christmas toys bought by monies out of the R.O. Employees 'Penny-a-Week' Charity Fund were distributed round the Children's Wards of local hospitals. Fund committee members, *left to right*, Jim Whitehouse, Frank Jellyman, Bill Telling, Arnold Onions and Doug Peach.

Peter Green from the A.T.V. To-day Programme interviews Annie Kimbley together with her 52 year old son Bill and Roy her 28 year old grandson. Annie was still happily pin pointing bolts at the age of 75, some sixty-two years after joining Nuts & Bolts (Darlaston). Three generations representing well over 100 years service with the same firm.

Downturn in the motor industry

The downturn in the British Motor Industry, rapid inflation and industrial relations problems throughout the country meant difficult times for everyone associated with manufacturing during the 70s. The R.O. Darlaston and King's Hill Factories were no exception. The R.O. strike of '76 closed the Darlaston factory for six weeks, nevertheless, up until 1979 there was a steady rate of production with scheduled deliveries being maintained to all customers.

Still dependant on the motor industry for 80% of its business, with 60% to 65% of that going to the newly formed British Leyland, R.O.s management felt smaller units at Darlaston would provide a greater degree of flexibility and specialisation. To enable this process to happen a decision was taken to divide Darlaston into two companies Rubery Owen **(Pressings and Fabrications)** Ltd. and Rubery Owen **(Wheels and Assemblies)** Ltd. The holding company made sure that both new companies had the most modern equipment in Europe to help them compete in difficult times.

Pressings and Fabrications

Hot Press Facilities.

Assembly and Sub-assembly.

Tool Design and Manufacture.

Inspection and Production Control.

Wheels and Assemblies

Motor Wheel Production.

Painting.

Quality Control/Wheel Testing.

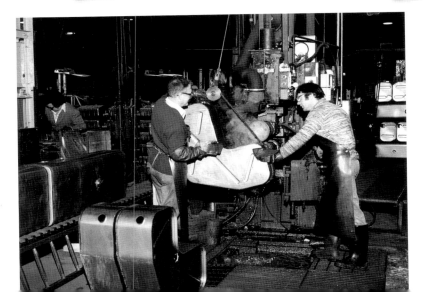

Fuel Tanks.

The R.O. stand at the 1968 Earls Court Motor Show.
The main emphasis of the exhibit being styled wheels.
'RO-Style wheels Change the Face of Motoring.'

A lady representative from Rover, demostrated the merits of the RO-Style wheel.

Motor Show 1980

In 1980 R.O.s Chairman David Owen responded to a question from Peter Colbourne (BBC Midlands) at the 2nd Motor Show at N.E.C. "It is really tough, demand has dropped on commercial vehicles, as well as cars. We have got a lot of people on short-time working but we're determined to try and keep going and weather it out."

One of the last photographs of the factory.

The last official photograph taken in 1982 with Sgt. George Peake on duty at the main Works entrance and the adjoining factory offices running down Booth Street. The connecting covered bridge was removed when the buildings were demolished shortly afterwards.

Taken from the parent company's buildinglooking out at the same area in 1985/6. A housing estate now occupies part of the former factory site, while the land in the foreground is being prepared for landscaping as open space with a children's play area.

The view in 2005

R.O. Holdings Ltd. the parent firm, now has two companies in the Darlaston Wednesbury area.

Rotech Laboratories Ltd. at Wednesbury provide a high-tech materials testing service, comprising mechanical, product finish, corrosion and non-destructive testing, in addition to chemical analysis and metallography. The laboratories also specialise in weld testing, fastener testing, and the investigation of service failures both in production and service.

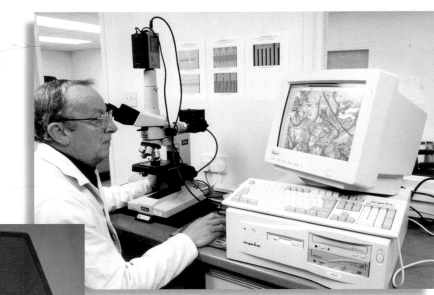

Investigating a service failure.

Corrosion tests.

Investigating tensile properties.

www.rotechlabs.co.uk